COMMERCE AND
BUSINESS MANAGEMENT

:: Author ::

RAJESHKUMAR A. SHRIMALI
(M.COM, B.ED, UGC NET, M.PHIL)

Published By

Green Flag Foundation
Sabarkantha, Gujrat-383210, India.
www.eternityzxy.com

ISBN 978-93-83579-60-0

First Publication: January, 2014

ISBN 978-93-83579-60-0

Price: Rs.150/-

Published by: Green Flag Foundation

Sabarkantha, Gujrat-383210, India

INDEX

BUSINESS ENVIRONMENT

- Meaning of Business Environment
- Importance of Business Environment
- Dimensions of Business Environment
- Major Elements of Social Environment
- Major Elements of Political Environment
- Economic Environment in India
- Government of India to announce economic reform were:
- Impact of Government Policy Changes on Business and Industry
- Elements of business environment

NATURE AND SIGNIFICANCE OF MANAGEMENT

INTRODUCTION

The successful top companies in India because of its quality of management. Management is required in all kinds of organisations whether they are manufacturing computers or hand-looms, trading in consumer goods or providing hairstyling services and even in non-business organisations. Let us take another example.

Tina is the branch manager of Reliance mart, an organisation that promotes the sales of Indian handloom and handicraft products while providing equitable employment to traditional artisans. Reliance mart sources its products from over 7500 craft persons and artisans across India. Planning the products is a difficult task that is done by a team of marketing and design experts to ensure that whatever is produced is according to market demand. These plans are then communicated by Tina to the rural artisans who actually implement them.

Reliance mart is a private limited company with several branches all over the country. It has a complex organisation structure in which actual production is in the hands of several skilled artisans and marketing is done by staff at branches such as the one managed by Tina. This means constantly providing direction and motivation to her employees. She also has to ensure that production is carried out according to plans in order to ensure regular sales.

A typical day in Tina's life consists of a series of interrelated and continuous functions. She has to plan a special festive collection for Diwali and Christmas. This means organising more funds and recruiting more artisans. She also has to regularly communicate with her suppliers to ensure that deadlines regarding delivery of goods are met. In the course of the day she meets customers for a general feedback Nature and Significance of Management and any suggestions that they may have.

Tina is the manager of Reliance mart. So is Nusli Wadia of Bombay Dyeing, Bill Gates of Microsoft, Shivani of HCL Enterprises, Indra Nooyi of Pepsico and the Principal of your school. They all manage organisations. Schools, hospitals, shops and large corporations are all organisations with diverse goals that are aimed at achieving something. No matter what the organisation is or what its goals might be, they all have something in common – management and managers.

You have observed that Tina's work as a manager consists of a series of different activities or functions aimed at achieving the goals of the organisation. These interconnected and interdependent functions are part of management. Successful organisations do not achieve their goals by chance but by following a deliberate process called 'management'.

Management is essential for all organisations big or small, profit or non-profit, services or manufacturing.

———————

Management is necessary so that individuals make their best contribution towards group objectives.

Management consists of a series of interrelated functions that are performed by all managers. Shivani, the CEO of HCL Enterprises performs all these functions and so does Tina at Reliance mart. Later in this chapter you will understand that although both of them are managers, they function at different levels in the organisation. The time spent by managers in different functions however is different. Managers at the top level spend more time in planning and organising than managers at lower levels of the organisation.

What is Management?

Management is a universal phenomenon. It is a very popular and widely used term. All organizations - business, political, cultural or social are involved in management because it is the management which helps and directs the various efforts towards a definite purpose. According to *Harold Koontz*, "Management is an art of getting things done through and with the people in formally organized groups. It is an art of creating an environment in which people can perform and individuals and can co-operate towards attainment of group goals". According to *F.W. Taylor*, "Management is an art of knowing what to do, when to do and see that it is done in the best and cheapest way".

Management is a purposive activity. It is something that

———————————

directs group efforts towards the attainment of certain pre - determined goals. It is the process of working with and through others to effectively achieve the goals of the organization, by efficiently using limited resources in the changing world. Of course, these goals may vary from one enterprise to another. E.g.: For one enterprise it may be launching of new products by conducting market surveys and for other it may be profit maximization by minimizing cost.

Management involves creating an internal environment: - It is the management which puts into use the various factors of production. Therefore, it is the responsibility of management to create such conditions which are conducive to maximum efforts so that people are able to perform their task efficiently and effectively. It includes ensuring availability of raw materials, determination of wages and salaries, formulation of rules & regulations etc.

Therefore, we can say that good management includes both being effective and efficient. Being effective means doing the appropriate task i.e, fitting the square pegs in square holes and round pegs in round holes. Being efficient means doing the task correctly, at least possible cost with minimum wastage of resources.

Management can be defined in detail in following categories :

1. Management as a Process
2. Management as an Activity

———————

3. Management as a Discipline
4. Management as a Group
5. Management as a Science
6. Management as an Art
7. Management as a Profession

CONCEPT

Management is a very popular term and has been used extensively for all types of activities and mainly for taking charge of different activities inane enterprise. As you have seen from the above example and case study that management is an activity which is necessary wherever there is a group of people working in an organisation. People in organisations are performing diverse tasks but they are all working towards the same goal. Management aims at guiding their efforts towards achieving a common objective — a goal. Thus, management has to see that tasks are completed and goals are achieved (i.e., effectiveness) with the least amount of resources at a minimum cost (i.e., efficiency).

Management, has therefore, been defined as a process of getting things done with the aim of achieving goals effectively and efficiently. We need to analyse this definition. There are certain terms which require elaboration. These are (a) process, (b) effectively, and (c) efficiently. Process in the definition means the primary functions or activities that management performs to get things done. These functions are planning, organising, staffing, directing and controlling which we will discuss later in the chapter and the book.

Being effective or doing work effectively basically means finishing the given task. Effectiveness in management is concerned with doing the right task, completing activities and achieving goals. In other words, it is concerned with the end result.

But it is not enough to just complete the tasks. There is another aspect also, i.e., being efficient or as we say doing work efficiently.

Efficiency means doing the task correctly and with minimum cost. There is a kind of cost-benefit analysis involved and the relationship between inputs and outputs. If by using less resources (i.e., the inputs) more benefits are derived (i.e., the outputs) then efficiency has increased. Efficiency is also increased when for the same benefit or outputs, fewer resources are used and less costs are incurred. Input resources are money, materials, equipment and persons required to do a particular task. Obviously, management is concerned with the efficient use of these resources, because they reduce costs and ultimately lead to higher profits.

Effectiveness versus Efficiency

These two terms are different but they are interrelated. For management, it is important to be both

_____

effective and efficient. Effectiveness and efficiency are two sides of the same coin. But these two aspects need to be balanced and management at times, has to compromise with efficiency. For example, it is easier to be effective and ignore efficiency i.e., complete the given task but at a high cost. Suppose, a company's target production is 5000 units in a year. To achieve this target the manager has to operate on double shifts due to power Nature and Significance of Management failure most of the time. The manager is able to produce 5000 units but at a higher production cost. In this case, the manager was effective but not so efficient, since for the same output, more inputs (labour cost, electricity costs) were used.

At times, a business may concentrate more on producing goods with fewer resources i.e., cutting down cost but not achieving the target production. Consequently, the goods do not reach the market and hence the demand for them declines and competitors enter the market. This is a case of being efficient but not effective since the goods did not reach the market.

Therefore, it is important for management to achieve goals (effectiveness) with minimum resources i.e., as efficiently as possible while maintaining a balance between effectiveness and efficiency. Usually high efficiency is associated with high effectiveness which is the aim of all managers. But undue emphasis on high efficiency without being effective is also not desirable. Poor management is due to both inefficiency and ineffectiveness.

———————

CHARACTERISTICS OF MANAGEMENT

After going through some of the definitions we find some elements that may be called the basic characteristics of management:

(i) **Management is a goal-oriented process:**

An organisation has a set of basic goals which are the basic reason for its existence. These should be simple and clearly stated. Different organisations have different goals. For example, the goal of a retail store may be to increase sales, but the goal of The Spastics Society of India is to impart education to children with special needs. Management unites the efforts of different individuals in the organisation towards achieving these goals.

(ii) **Management is all pervasive:**

The activities involved in managing an enterprise are common to all organisations whether economic, social or political. A petrol pump needs to be managed as much as a hospital or a school. What managers do in India, the USA, Germany or Japan is the same. How they do it may be quite different. This difference is due to the differences in culture, tradition and history.

(iii) **Management is multidimensional:**

Management is a complex activity that has three main dimensions. These are:

(a) *Management of work:* All organisations exist for the performance of some work. In a factory, a product is

———————

manufactured, in a garment store a customer's need is satisfied and in a hospital a patient is treated. Management translates this work in terms of goals to be achieved and assigns the means to achieve it. This is done in terms of problems to be solved, decisions to be made, plans to be established, budgets to be prepared, responsibilities to be assigned and authority to be delegated.

(b) *Management of people:* Human resources or people are an organisation's greatest asset. Despite all developments in technology "getting work done through people" is still a major task for the manager. The task of management is to make people work towards achieving the organisation's goals, by making their strengths effective and their weaknesses irrelevant.

(c) *Management of operations:* No matter what the organisation, it has some basic product or service to provide in order to survive. This requires a production process which entails the flow of input material and the technology for transforming this input into the desired output for consumption. This is interlinked with both the management of work and the management of people.

(iv)   **Management is a continuous process:**

The process of management is a series of continuous, composite, but separate functions (planning, organising, directing, staffing and controlling). These functions are simultaneously performed by all managers all the time. You may have observed that Tina at Reliance mart performs several different tasks in a single day. Some days she may

———————————

spend more time in planning a future exhibition and on another day she may spend time in sorting out an employee's problem. The task of a manager consists of an ongoing series of functions.

(v)   **Management is a group activity:**

An organisation is a collection of diverse individuals with different needs. Every member of the group has a different purpose for joining the organisation but as members of the organisation they work towards fulfilling the common organisational goal. This requires team work and coordination of individual effort in a common direction. At the same time management should enable all its members to grow and develop as needs and opportunities change.

(vi)   **Management is a dynamic function:**

Management is a dynamic function and has to adapt itself to the changing environment. An organisation interacts with its external environment which consists of various social, economic and political factors. In order to be successful, an organisation must change itself and its goals according to the needs of the environment. You probably know that McDonalds, the fast food giant made major changes in its menu to be able to survive in the Indian market.

(vii)   Management is an intangible force:

Management is an intangible force that cannot be seen but its presence can be felt in the way the organisation functions. The effect of management is noticeable in an organisation where targets are met according to plans,

———————

employees are happy and satisfied, and there is orderliness instead of chaos.

OBJECTIVES OF MANAGEMENT

Management seeks to achieve certain objectives which are the desired result of any activity. They must be derived from the basic purpose of the business. In any organisation there are different objectives and management has to achieve all objectives in an effective and efficient manner. Objectives can be classified into organisational objectives, social objectives and personal or individual objectives.

(i) Organisational Objectives:

Management is responsible for setting and achieving objectives for the organisation. It has to achieve a variety of objectives in all areas considering the interest of all stakeholders including, shareholders, employees, customers and the government. The main objective of any organisation should be to utilise human and material resources to the maximum possible advantage, i.e., to fulfill the economic objectives of a business. These are survival, profit and growth.

Survival: The basic objectives of any business is survival. Management must strive to ensure the survival of the organisation. In order to survive, an organisation must earn enough revenues to cover costs.

Profit: Mere survival is not enough for business. Management has to ensure that the organisation makes a profit. Profit provides a vital incentive for the continued successful operation of the enterprise. Profit is essential for covering costs and risks of the business.

Growth: A business needs to add to its prospects in the long run, for this it is important for the business to grow. To remain in the industry, management must exploit fully the growth potential of the organisation. Growth of a business can be measured in terms of sales volume increase in the number of employees, the number of products or the increase in capital investment, etc. There can be other indicators of growth.

(ii)   **Social objectives:**

It involves the creation of benefit for society. As a part of society, every organisation whether it is 10 Business Studies

business or non-business, has a social obligation to fulfill. This refers to consistently creating economic value for various constituents of society. This includes using environmental friendly methods of production, giving employment opportunities to the disadvantaged sections of society and providing basic amenities like schools and crèches to employees. The box given below illustrates how a company can fulfill its social responsibility.

(iv)   **Personal objectives:**

Organisations are made up of people who have different personalities, backgrounds, experiences and objectives. They all become part of the organisation to satisfy their diverse needs. These vary from financial needs

_____

such as competitive salaries and perks, social needs such as peer recognition and higher level needs such as personal growth and development. Management has to reconcile personal goals with organisational objectives for harmony in the organisation.

IMPORTANCE OF MANAGEMENT

Having understood that management is a universal activity that is integral to any organisation we now examine some of the reasons that have made management so important:

(i) **Management helps in achieving group goals:**

Management is required not for itself but for achieving the goals of the organisation. The task of a manager is to give a common direction to the individual effort in achieving the overall goal of the organisation.

(ii) **Management increases efficiency:**

The aim of a manager is to reduce costs and increase productivity through better planning, organising, directing, staffing and controlling the activities of the organisation.

(iii) **Management creates a dynamic organisation:**

All organisations have to function in an environment which is constantly changing. It is generally seen that individuals in an organisation resist change as it often means moving from a familiar, secure environment into a newer and more challenging one. Management helps people adapt to these changes so that the organisation is able to maintain its competitive edge.

(iv) **Management helps in achieving personal objectives:**

A manager motivates and leads his team in such a manner that individual members are able to achieve personal goals while contributing to the overall organisational objective. Through motivation and leadership the management helps individuals to develop team spirit, cooperation and commitment to group success.

(v) **Management helps in the development of society:**

An organisation has multiple objectives to serve the purpose of the different groups that constitute it. In the process of fulfilling all these, management helps in the development of the organisation and through that it helps in the development of society. It helps to provide good quality products and services, creates employment opportunities, adopts new techno-logy for the greater good of the people and leads the path towards growth and development.

NATURE OF MANAGEMENT

Management is as old as civilisation. Although modern organisations are 1Business Studies of recent origin, organised activity has existed since the time of the ancient civilisations. In fact, organisations may be considered the distinguishing feature that separated civilised society from uncivilised ones. The earliest management practices were a set of rules and regulations that grew out of the experiences of governmental and commercial activities. The development of trade and commerce gradually led to the development of management principles and practices.

The term 'management' today has several different connotations that highlight the different aspects of its nature. The study of management has evolved over a period of time along with the modern organisations; based both on the experience and practice of managers and a set of theoretical relationships. Over a period of time, it has grown into a dynamic subject with its own special characteristics. However, one question that needs to be addressed pertaining to the nature of management is whether it is a science or an art or both? In order to answer this let us examine the features of both science and art to see how far management fulfills them.

MANAGEMENT AS AN ART

What is art? Art is the skillful and personal application of existing knowledge to achieve desired results. It can be acquired through study, observation and experience. Since art is concerned with personal application of knowledge some kind of ingenuity and creativity is required to practice the basic principles learnt. The basic features of an art are as follows:

(i) **Existence of theoretical knowledge:**

_____

Art presupposes the existence of certain theoretical knowledge. Experts in their respective areas have derived certain basic principles which are applicable to a particular form of art. For example, literature on dancing, public speaking, acting or music is widely recognised.

(ii) **Personalised application:**

The use of this basic knowledge varies from individual to individual. Art, therefore, is a very personalised concept. For example, two dancers, two speakers, two actors, or two writers will always differ in demonstrating their art.

(iii) **Based on practice and creativity:**

All art is practical. Art involves the creative practice of existing theoretical knowledge. We know that all music is based on seven basic notes. However, what makes the composition of a musician unique or different is his use of these notes in a creative manner that is entirely his own interpretation.

Management can be said to be an art since it satisfies the following criteria:

(i) A successful manager practices the art of management in the Nature and Significance of Management 1day-to-day job of managing an enterprise based on study, observation and experience. There is a lot of literature available in various areas of management like marketing, finance and human resources which the manager has to specialise in. There is existence of theoretical knowledge.

(ii) There are various theories of management, as propounded by many management thinkers, which prescribe

———————

certain universal principles. A manager applies these scientific methods and body of knowledge to a given situation, an issue or a problem, in his own unique manner. A good manager works through a combination of practice, creativity, imagination, initiative and innovation. A manager achieves perfection after long practice. Students of management also apply these principles differently depending on how creative they are.

(iii)   A manager applies this acquired knowledge in a personalised and skillful manner in the light of the realities of a given situation. He is involved in the activities of the organisation, studies critical situations and formulates his own theories for use in a given situation. This gives rise to different styles of management

The best managers are committed and dedicated individuals; highly trained and educated, with personal qualities such as ambition, self-motivation, creativity and imagination, a desire for development of the self and the organisation they belong to. All management practices are based on the same set of principles; what distinguishes a successful manager from a less successful one is the ability to put these principles into practice.

MANAGEMENT AS A PROCESS

As a process, management refers to a series of inter-related functions. It is the process by which management creates, operates and directs purposive organization through systematic, coordinated and co-operated human efforts, according to George R. Terry, "Management is a distinct process consisting of planning, organizing, actuating and controlling, performed to determine and accomplish stated objective by the use of human beings and other resources". As a process, management consists of three aspects:

1.   Management is a social process - Since human factor is most important among the other factors, therefore management is concerned with developing relationship among people. It is the duty of management to make interaction between people - productive and useful for obtaining organizational goals.

2.   Management is an integrating process - Management undertakes the job of bringing together human physical and financial resources so as to achieve organizational purpose. Therefore, is an important function to bring harmony between various factors.

3.   Management is a continuous process - It is a never ending process. It is concerned with constantly identifying the problem and solving them by taking adequate steps. It is an on-going process.

MANAGEMENT AS AN ACTIVITY

Like various other activities performed by human beings such as writing, playing, eating, cooking etc, management is also an activity because a manager is one who accomplishes the objectives by directing the efforts of others. According to

Koontz, "Management is what a manager does". Management as an activity includes -

1.   Informational activities - In the functioning of business enterprise, the manager constantly has to receive and give information orally or in written. A communication link has to be maintained with subordinates as well as superiors for effective functioning of an enterprise.

2.   Decisional activities - Practically all types of managerial activities are based on one or the other types of decisions. Therefore, managers are continuously involved in decisions of different kinds since the decision made by one manager becomes the basis of action to be taken by other managers. (E.g. Sales Manager is deciding the media & content of advertising).

3.   Inter-personal activities - Management involves achieving goals through people. Therefore, managers have to interact with superiors as well as the sub-ordinates. They must maintain good relations with them. The inter-personal activities include with the sub-ordinates and taking care of the problem. (E.g. Bonuses to be given to the sub-ordinates).

MANAGEMENT AS A DISCIPLINE

Management as a discipline refers to that branch of knowledge which is connected to study of principles & practices of basic administration. It specifies certain code of conduct to be followed by the manager & also various methods for managing resources efficiently.

_____

Management as a discipline specifies certain code of conduct for managers & indicates various methods of managing an enterprise. Management is a course of study which is now formally being taught in the institutes and universities after completing a prescribed course or by obtaining degree or diploma in management, a person can get employment as a manager.

Any branch of knowledge that fulfils following two requirements is known as discipline:

1. There must be scholars & thinkers who communicate relevant knowledge through research and publications.

2. The knowledge should be formally imparted by education and training programmes.

Since management satisfies both these problems, therefore it qualifies to be a discipline. Though it is comparatively a new discipline but it is growing at a faster pace.

MANAGEMENT AS A GROUP

Management as a group refers to all those persons who perform the task of managing an enterprise. When we say that management of ABC & Co. is good, we are referring to a group of people those who are managing. Thus as a group technically speaking, management will include all managers from chief executive to the first - line managers (lower-level managers). But in common practice management includes only top management i.e. Chief Executive, Chairman, General Manager, Board of Directors etc. In other words, those who are concerned with making important decisions, these persons enjoy the authorities to use resources to accomplish organizational objectives & also responsibility to for their efficient utilization.

Management as a group may be looked upon in 2 different ways:

1. All managers taken together.

2. Only the top management

The interpretation depends upon the context in which these terms are used. Broadly speaking, there are 3 types of managers -

1. Patrimonial / Family Manager: Those who have become managers by virtue of their being owners or relatives of the owners of company.

2. Professional Managers: Those who have been appointed on account of their specialized knowledge and degree.

3. Political Managers / Civil Servants: Those who manage public sector undertakings.

Managers have become a part of elite group of society as they enjoy higher standard of living in the society.

MANAGEMENT AS A SCIENCE

Science is a systematised body of knowledge that explains certain general truths or the operation of general laws. The basic features of science are as follows:

(i) **Systematised body of knowledge:**

_____

Science is a systematic body of knowledge. Its principles are based on a cause and effect relationship. For example, the phenomenon of an apple falling from a tree towards the ground is explained by the law of gravity.

(ii)   Principles based on experimentation:

Scientific principles are first developed through observation and then tested through repeated experimentation under controlled conditions.

(iii)   Universal validity:

Scientific principles have universal validity and application. Based on the above features, we can say that management has some characteristics of science.

(i) Management has a systematised body of knowledge. It has its own theory and principles that have developed over a period of time, but it also draws on other disciplines such as Economics, Sociology, Psychology and Mathematics. Like all other organised activity, management has its own vocabulary of terms and concepts. For example, all of us discuss sports like cricket and soccer using a common vocabulary. The players also use these terms to communicate with each other. Similarly managers need to communicate with one another with the help of a common vocabulary for a better understanding of their work situation.

(ii) The principles of management have evolved over a period of time based on repeated experimentation and observation in different types of organisations. However, since management deals with human beings and human behaviour, the outcomes of these experiments are not capable of being accurately predicted or replicated. Therefore, management can be called an inexact science. Despite these limitations, management scholars have been able to identify general principles of management. For example, scientific management principles by F.W. Taylor and Functional Management principles by Henri Fayol.

(iii)   Since the principles of management are not as exact as the principles of science, their application and use is not universal. They have to be modified according to a given situation. However, they provide managers with certain standardised techniques that can be used in different situations. These principles are also used for training and development of managers.

You must have understood from the foregoing discussion that management has features of both art and science. The practice of management is an art. However, managers can work better if their practice is based on the principles of management. These principles constitute the science of management. Management as an art and a science are therefore not mutually exclusive, but complement each other.

MANAGEMENT AS A PROFESSION

You have understood so far that all forms of organised activity need to be managed. You would also have observed that organisations look for individuals with specific qualifications and experience to manage them. It has also been observed that there has been an increase in the corporate form of business on the one hand and Business Studies increasing emphasis on managed business concerns. Does this imply that management is a profession? To answer this question let us examine the salient features of a profession and see whether management satisfies them.

A profession has the following characteristics:

(i)   **Well-defined body of know-ledge**:

All professions are based on a well-defined body of knowledge that can be acquired through instruction.

(ii)   Restricted entry:

The entry to a profession is restricted through an examination or through acquiring an educational degree. For example, to become a chartered accountant in India a candidate has to clear a specified examination conducted by the Institute of Chartered Accountants of India.

(iii)   Professional association:

All professions are affiliated to a professional association which regulates entry, grants certificate of practice and formulates and enforces a code of conduct. To be able to practice in India lawyers have to become members of the Bar Council which regulates and controls their activities.

(iv)   Ethical code of conduct:

All professions are bound by a code of conduct which guides the behavior of its members. All doctors, for example, take the oath of ethical practice at the time they enter the profession.

(v)   Service motive:

The basic motive of a profession is to serve their client's interests by rendering dedicated and committed service. The task of a lawyer is to ensure that his client gets justice.

Management does not meet the exact criteria of a profession. However, it does have some of the features of a profession:

(i) All over the world there is marked growth in management as a discipline. It is based on a systematic body of knowledge comprising well-defined principles based on a variety of business situations. This knowledge can be acquired at different colleges and professional institutes and through a number of books and journals. The subject of management is taught at different institutions. Some of these have been set up with the specific purpose of providing management education such as the Indian Institutes of Management (IIMs) in India. Entry to different institutes is usually through an examination.

(ii) There is no restriction on anyone being designated or appointed as manager in any business enterprise. Anyone can be called a manager irrespective of the educational qualifications possessed. Nature and Significance of Management Unlike professions such as medicine or law which require a practicing doctor or lawyer to possess valid degrees, nowhere in the world is it mandatory for a manager to possess any such specific degree. But professional knowledge and training is considered to be a desirable

_____

qualification, since there is greater demand for those who possess degrees or diplomas from reputed institutions. Therefore, as such the second criterion has not been strictly met.

(iii) There are several associations of practising managers in India, like the AIMA (All India Management Association) that has laid down a code of conduct to regulate the activities of their members. There is, however, no compulsion for managers to be members of such an association nor does it have any statutory backing.

(iv) The basic purpose of management is to help the organisation achieve its stated goal. This may be profit maximisation for a business enterprise and service for a hospital. However, profit maximisation as the objective of management does not hold true and is fast changing. Therefore, if an organisation has a good management team that is efficient and effective it automatically serves society by providing good quality products at reasonable prices.

LEVELS OF MANAGEMENT

Shivani and Tina are both managers of an enterprise. Shivani is the CEO of HCL and Tina is a branch manager at Reliance mart. They manage their enterprise at different levels. Management is a universal term used for certain functions performed by individuals in an enterprise who are bound together in a hierarchy of relationships. Every individual in the hierarchy is responsible for successful completion of a particular task. To be able to fulfill that responsibility he is assigned a certain amount of authority or the right to take a decision. This authority-responsibility relationship binds individuals as superiors and subordinates and gives rise to different levels in an organisation. Generally speaking there are three levels in the hierarchy of an organisation.

(i) **Top Management:** They consists of the senior-most executives of the organisation by whatever name they are called. They are usually referred to as the chairman, the chief executive officer, chief operating officer, president and vice-president. Top management is a team consisting of managers from different functional levels. Their basic task is to integrate diverse elements and coordinate the activities of different departments Business Studies according to the overall objectives of the organisation. These top level managers are responsible for the welfare and survival of the organisation. They analyse the business environment and its implications for the survival of the firm. They formulate overall organisational goals and strategies for their achievement. They are responsible for all the activities of the business and for its impact on society. The job of the top manager is complex and stressful, demanding long hours and commitment to the organisation.

(ii)   **Middle Management:**

is the link between top and lower level managers. They are subordinate to top managers and superior to the first line managers. They are usually known as division heads, operations manager or plant superintendent. Middle management is responsible for implementing and controlling plans and strategies developed by top management. At the same time they are responsible for all the activities of first line managers. Their main task is to carry out the plans formulated by the top managers. For this they need to: (i) interpret the policies framed by top management, (ii) ensure that their department has the necessary personnel, (iii) assign necessary duties and responsibilities to them, (iv) motivate them to achieve desired objectives, and (v) co-operate with other departments for smooth functioning of the organisation. At the same time they are responsible for all the activities of first line managers.

(iv)   Supervisory or Operational Management:

Foremen and supervisors comprise the lower level in the hierarchy of the organisation. Supervisors directly oversee the efforts of the workforce. Their authority and responsibility is limited according to the plans drawn by the top management. Supervisory management plays a very important role in the organisation since they interact with the actual work force and pass on instructions of the middle management to the workers. Through their efforts quality of output is maintained, wastage of materials is minimised and safety standards are maintained. The quality of workmanship and the quantity of output depends on the hard work, discipline and loyalty of the workers.

FUNCTIONS OF MANAGEMENT

Management is described as the process of planning, organising, directing and controlling the efforts of organisational members and of using organisational resources to achieve specific goals.

Planning is the function of determining in advance what is to be done and who is to do it. This implies setting goals in advance and developing a way of achieving them efficiently and effectively. In Tina's organisation the objective is procurement and sale of traditional Indian handloom and handicraft items. They sell fabrics, furnishings, readymades and household items made out of traditional Indian fabrics. Tina has to decide quantities, variety, colour and texture of all the above and then allocate resources for their purchase from different suppliers or for their inhouse development. Planning cannot prevent problems, but it can predict them and prepare contingency plans to deal with them if and when they occur.

Organising is the management function of assigning duties, grouping tasks, establishing authority and allocating resources required to carry out a specific plan. Once a specific plan has been established for the accomplishment of an organisational goal, the organising function examines the activities and resources required to implement the plan. It determines what activities and resources are required. It decides who will do a particular task, where it will be done, and when it will be done. Organising involves the grouping of the required tasks into manageable departments or work units and the establishment of authority and reporting relationships within the organisational hierarchy. Proper organisational techniques help in the accomplishment of work and promote both the efficiency of operations and the effectiveness of results. Different kinds of business require different structures according to the nature of work. You will read more about this in a later chapter.

Staffing simply stated, is finding the right people for the right job. A very important aspect of management is to make sure that the right people with the right qualifications are available at the right places and times to accomplish the goals of the organisation. This is also known as the human resource function and it involves activities such as recruitment, selection, placement and training of personnel. Infosys Technologies which develops software needs systems analysts and programmers, whereas Reliance mart needs a team of designers and craftspeople.

Directing involves leading, influencing and motivating employees to perform the tasks assigned to them. This requires establishing an atmosphere that encourages employees to do their best. Motivation and leadership are two key Nature and Significance of Management components of direction. Motivating workers means simply creating an environment that makes them want to work. Leadership is influencing others to do what the leader wants them to do. A good manager directs through praise and criticism in such a way that it brings out the best in the employee. Tina's design team developed some prints for bedcovers in bright colours on silk. Although they looked

———————

very impressive, the use of silk made the product too expensive for the average customer. Praising their effort, Tina suggested that they keep the silk bedcovers for special occasions like Diwali and Christmas and offer the cotton bedcovers on a regular basis.

Controlling is the management function of monitoring organisational performance towards the attainment of organisational goals. The task of controlling involves establishing standards of performance, measuring current performance, comparing this with established standards and taking corrective action where any deviation is found. Here management must determine what activities and outputs are critical to success, how and where they can be measured and who should have the authority to take corrective action. When Tina discovered that her team of designers had produced bedcovers that were more expensive than they had planned to sell, she decided to change the fabric to keep costs in check.

The various functions of a manager are usually discussed in the order given above, suggesting that a manager first plans, then organises, puts staff in position, then directs, and finally controls. In reality, managers are rarely able to carry out these functions in isolation. The activities of a manager are interrelated and it is often difficult to pinpoint where one ended and the other began.

COORDINATION - THE ESSENCE OF MANAGEMENT

You have understood by now that a manager has to perform five interrelated functions in the process of managing an organisation which is a system made up of different interlinked and interdependent subsystems. A manager has to link these diverse groups towards the achievement of a common goal. The process by which a manager synchronises the activities of different departments is known as coordination.

Coordination is the force that binds all the other functions of management. It is the common thread that runs through all activities such as purchase, production, sales, and finance to ensure continuity in the working of the organisation. Coordination is sometimes considered a separate function of management. It is however, the Business Studies essence of management, for achieving harmony among individual efforts towards the accomplishment of group goals. Each managerial function is an exercise contributing individually to coordination. Coordination is implicit and inherent in all functions of an organisation.

The process of coordinating the activities of an organisation begins at the planning stage itself. Top management plans for the entire organisation. According to these plans the organisational structure is developed and staffed. In order to ensure that these plans are executed according to plans directing is required. Any discrepancies between actual and realised activities are then taken care of at the stage of controlling. It is through the process of coordination that a manager ensures the orderly arrangement of individual and group efforts to ensure unity of action in the realisation of common objectives. Coordination therefore involves synchronisation of the different actions or efforts of the various units of an organisation. This provides the requisite amount, quality, timing and sequence of efforts which ensures that planned objectives are achieved with a minimum of conflict.

NATURE OF COORDINATION

The definitions given above highlight the following features of coordination:

(i) Coordination integrates group efforts: Coordination unifies unrelated or diverse interests into purposeful work activity. It gives a common focus to group effort to ensure that performance is as it was planned and scheduled.

(ii) Coordination ensures unity of action: The purpose of coordination is to secure unity of action in the realisation of a common purpose. It acts as the binding force between departments and ensures that all action is aimed at achieving the goals of the organisation. You have observed that at Reliance mart, the production and sales department have to coordinate their work, so that production takes place according to the demand in the market.

(iii) Coordination is a continuous process:

Coordination is not a one-time function but a continuous process. It begins at the planning stage and

———————

continues till controlling. Tina plans her winter collection in the month of June itself. She has to then ensure that there is adequate workforce and continuously monitor whether production is proceeding according to plans. Her marketing department also has to be briefed in time to prepare their promotional and advertising campaigns.

(iv) Coordination is an all pervasive function: Coordination is required at all levels of management due to the interdependent nature of activities of various departments. It integrates the efforts of different departments and different levels. The purchase, production and sales departmental efforts have to be coordinated by Tina for achieving organisational objectives harmoniously. The purchase department is responsible for procuring fabric. This then becomes the basis of the activities of the production department and finally sales can take place. If fabric purchased is of an inferior quality or is not according to the specifications of the production department, further sales will also decline. In the absence of coordination there is overlapping and chaos instead of harmony and integration of activities.

(v) Coordination is the responsibility of all managers: Coordination is the function of every manager in the organisation. Top level managers need to coordinate with their subordinates to ensure that the overall policies for the organisation are duly carried out. Middle level management coordinates with both the top level and first line managers.

————————

Operational level management coordinates the activities of its workers to ensure that work proceeds according to plans.

(vi) Coordination is a deliberate function: A manager has to coordinate the efforts of different people in a conscious and deliberate manner. Even where members of a department willingly cooperate and work, coordination gives a direction to that willing spirit. Cooperation in the absence of coordination may lead to wasted effort and coordination without cooperation may lead to dissatisfaction among employees.

Coordination, therefore, is not a separate function of management, but it's very essence. For an organisation to effectively and efficiently achieve its objectives coordination is required. Like a thread in a garland, coordination is a part of all management functions.

Management in the Twenty-first Century

Even as you read this chapter, the organisation and its management are changing. As boundaries between cultures and nations get blurred and new communication technology makes it possible to think of the world as a 'global village', the scope of international and intercultural relationships is rapidly expanding. The modern organisation is a global organisation that has to be managed in a global perspective. What does this imply? Business Studies work environment – in terms of multiple time-zones, understanding of client's priorities based on the business cycles that the client's business operates in, understanding and adapting to the processes and methodologies the client is familiar with. Finally this function also includes customer expectation management, where the functional manager has to coordinate activities in India and in USA/Europe according to the customer's priorities, communicate what is possible and what is not possible, and accordingly also manage the expectations and satisfaction levels of his own employees.

- **In the capacity of the 'business leader'** – the global manager has to be alive to changing business situations and customer priorities – he has to keep track of the trends in outsourcing – and have the ability to envision upcoming opportunities as well as potential risks. For example, having a firm grip on the changing legislations on outsourcing is critical for a business manager to understand if his current clients are going to continue giving him business. The global manager also needs to be extremely responsive in what customers may perceive as gaps between the operating environment in India vis-à-vis their own countries. He has to position the advantages that outsourcing to India offers – in terms of lowered costs and access to a wide talent-base, while expertly addressing concerns on weak areas like infrastructure in India.

What do all these mean for a global manager today?

To summarise, a global manager today is one who possesses what can be termed as 'hard' types of skills as well as 'softer' types of skills. Managers who understand analysis, strategy, engineering, and technology are still going to be needed, but extremely critical to global success are people who understand how teams work, how organisations work, how people are motivated.

A manager who really understands different cultures should be able to work in a West European, non-English speaking country, then move to a developing country like Malaysia or Kenya, and then be transferred to an office based in New York, USA, and be almost immediately productive in all three places.

It can thus be understood that the role of a global manager has evolved in much the same way that the global industry and economy have evolved. It has changed from being a single dimensional role in a defined business context, to being a multi-faceted role that calls for a diverse combination of technical skills, soft management and people skills, and the ability to imbibe and learn different cultural experiences.

PRINCIPLES OF MANAGEMENT

It is clear from the foregoing case that managerial pursuits at Toyota Motor Corporation are driven by principles that serve as broad guidelines for stating the vision as well as the ways to achieve it. Similarly, many other business enterprises have followed various principles in their working over a period of time. A number of management thinkers, and writers have also studied principles of management from time-to-time. In fact, there is a long history of management thought. Management principles have evolved and are in the continuous process of evolution.

———————

You can see that the evolution of management thought has been very fascinating. In this chapter we will study the contributions of Fredrick Winslow Taylor and Henri Fayol who as you have read are associated with the classical management theory. Both of them contributed immensely towards the study of management as a discipline. Whereas F.W. Taylor was an American mechanical engineer, Henri Fayol was a French mining engineer. Taylor gave the concept of 'Scientific Management' whereas Fayol emphasised 'Administrative Principles'.

But before we go into the details of their contributions let us study the meaning of the principles of management.

Principles of Management: The Concept

A managerial principle is a broad and general guideline for decision-making and behaviour. For example while deciding about promotion of an employee one manager may consider seniority, whereas the other may follow the principle of merit.

One may distinguish principles of management from those of pure science. Management principles are not as rigid as principles of pure science. They deal with human behaviour and, thus, are to be applied creatively given the demands of the situation. Human behaviour is never static and so also technology, which affects business. Hence all the principles have to keep pace with these changes. For example, in the absence of Information and Communications Technology (ICT), a manager could oversee only a small work force that too within a narrow geographical space. The advent of ICT has expanded the capability of the managers to preside over large business empires spread across the globe. Infosys headquarters in Bangalore boast of the Asia's largest flat screen in their conference room from where their managers can interact with their employees and customers in all parts of the world.

In developing an understanding of the meaning of principles of management, it is also useful to know what these are not. The principles of management should be distinguished from techniques of management. Techniques are procedures or methods, which involve a series of steps to be taken to accomplish desired goals. Principles are guidelines to take decisions or actions while practicing techniques. Likewise, principles should also be understood as being distinct from values. Values are something, which are acceptable or desirable. They have moral connotations. Principles are basic truths or guidelines for behaviour. Values are general rules for behaviour of individuals in society formed through common practice whereas principles of management are formed after research in work situations, which are technical in nature. However, while practicing principles of management values cannot be neglected, as businesses have to fulfill social and ethical responsibilities towards society.

Nature of Principles of Management

———————

By nature is meant qualities and characteristics of anything. Principles are general propositions, which are applicable when certain conditions are present. These have been developed on the basis of observation and experimentation as well as personal experiences of the managers. Depending upon how they are derived and how effective they are in explaining and predicting managerial behaviour, they contribute towards the development of management both as a science and as an art. Derivation of these principles may be said to be a matter of science and their creative application may be regarded as an art. These principles lend credibility of a learnable and teachable discipline to the practice of management. As such, ascent to managerial position may not be a matter of birth, but a matter of requisite qualifications. Clearly, management principles have gained importance with increasing professionalization of management.

These principles are guidelines to action. They denote a cause and effect relationship. While functions of management viz., Planning, Organising, Staffing, Directing and Controlling are the actions to be taken while practicing management, Principles help managers to take decisions while performing these functions. The following points summarise the nature of principles of management.

(i) Universal applicability:

The principles of management are intended to apply to all types of organisations, business as well as non-business, small as well large, public sector as well as private sector, manufacturing as well as the services sectors. However, the extent of their applicability would vary with the nature of the organisation, business activity, scale of operations and the like. For example, for greater productivity, work should be divided into small tasks and each employee should be trained to perform his/her specialised job. This principle is applicable to a government office where there is a diary/dispatch clerk whose job is to receive and send mail or documents, a data entry operator whose task is to input data on the computer, a peon and an officer etc. This principle is also applicable to a limited company where there are separate departments like Production, Finance, Marketing and Research and Development etc. Extent of division of work, however, may vary from case to case.

(ii) General guidelines:

The principles are guidelines to action but do not provide readymade, straitjacket solutions to all managerial problems. This is so because real business situations are very complex and dynamic and are a result of many factors. However, the importance of principles cannot be underestimated because even a small guideline helps to solve a given problem. For example, in dealing with a situation of conflict between two departments, a manager may emphasis the primacy of the overall goals of the organisation.

(iii) Formed by practice and experimentation:

———————

The principles of management are formed by experience and collective wisdom of managers as well as experimentation. For example, it is a matter of common experience that discipline is indispensable for accomplishing any purpose. This principle finds mention in management theory. On the other hand, in order to remedy the problem of fatigue of workers in the factory, an experiment may be conducted to see the effect of improvement of physical conditions to reduce stress.

(iv)   Flexi bile:

The principles of management are not rigid prescriptions, which have to be followed absolutely. They are flexible and can be modified by the manager when the situation 36 Business Studies so demands. They give the manager enough discretion to do so. For example, the degree of concentration of authority (centralisation) or its dispersal (decentralisation) will depend upon the situations and circumstances of each enterprise. Moreover individual principles are like different tools serving different purposes, the manager has to decide which tool to use under what circumstances.

(v)   Mainly behavioural:

Management principles aim at influencing behaviour of human beings. Therefore, principles of management are mainly behavioural in nature. It is not that these principles do not pertain to things and phenomenon at all, it is just a matter of emphasis. Moreover, principles enable a better understanding of the relationship between human and material resources in accomplishing organisational purposes. For example, while planning the layout of a factory, orderliness would require that workflows are matched by flow of materials and movement of men.

(vi) Cause and effect relationships:

The principles of management are intended to establish relationship between cause and effect so that they can be used in similar situations in a large number of cases. As such, they tell us if a particular principle was applied in a particular situation, what would be its likely effect. The principles of management are less than perfect since they mainly apply to human behaviour. In real life, situations are not identical. So, accurate cause and effect relationships may be difficult to establish. However, principles of management assist managers in establishing these relationships to some extent and are therefore useful. In situations of emergencies, it is desirable that someone takes charge and others just follow. But in situations requiring cross-functional expertise, such as setting up of a new factory, more participative approach to decision-making would be advisable.

(vii) Contingent:

The application of principles of management is contingent or dependent upon the prevailing situation at a particular point of time. The application of principles has to be changed as per requirements. For example, employees deserve fair and just remuneration. But what is just and fair is determined by multiple factors. They include contribution

———————————

of the employee, paying capacity of the employer and also prevailing wage rate for the occupation under consideration. a part of management principles directly or indirectly. Now you can see the significance of these principles.

Significance of Principles of Management

The principles of management derive their significance from their utility. They provide useful insights to managerial behaviour and influence managerial practices. Managers may apply these principles to fulfill their tasks and responsibilities. Principles guide managers in taking and implementing decisions. It may be appreciated that everything worthwhile is governed by an underlying principle. The quest of the management theorists has been and should be to unearth the underlying principles with a view to using these under repetitive circumstances as a matter of management habit. The significance of principles of management can be discussed in terms of the following points:

(i) Providing managers with useful insights into reality: The principles of management provide the managers with useful insights into real world situations. Adherence to these principles will add to their knowledge, ability and understanding of managerial situations and circumstances. It will also enable managers to learn from past mistakes and conserve time by solving recurring problems quickly. As such management principles increase managerial efficiency. For example, a manager can leave routine decision-making to his subordinates and deal with exceptional situations which require her/his expertise by following the principles of delegation.

(ii) Optimum utilization of resources and effective administration: Resources both human and material available with the company are limited. They have to be put to optimum use. By optimum use we mean that the resources should be put to use in such a manner that they should give maximum benefit with minimum cost. Principles equip the managers to foresee the cause and effect relationships of their decisions and actions. As such the wastages associated with a trial-and-error approach can be overcome. Effective administration necessitates impersonalisation of managerial conduct so that managerial power is used with due discretion. Principles of management limit the boundary of managerial discretion so that their decisions may be free from personal prejudices and biases. For example, in deciding the annual budgets for different departments, rather than personal preferences, managerial discretion is bounded by the principle of contribution to organisational objectives.

(iii) Scientific decisions: Decisions must be based on facts, thoughtful and justifiable in terms of the intended purposes. They must be timely, realistic and subject to measurement and evaluation. Management principles help in thoughtful decision-making. They emphasise logic rather

———————

than blind faith. Management decisions taken on the basis of principles are free from bias and prejudice. They are based on the objective assessment of the situation.

(iv) Meeting changing environment requirements: Although the principles are in the nature of general guidelines but they are modified and as such help managers to meet changing requirements of the environment. You have already studied that management principles are flexible to adapt to dynamic business environment. For example, management principles emphasise division of work and specialisation. In modern times this principle has been extended to the entire business whereby companies are specialising in their core competency and divesting non-core businesses. In this context, one may cite the decision of Hindustan Lever Limited in divesting non-core businesses of chemicals and seeds. Some companies are outsourcing their non-core activities like share-transfer management and advertising to outside agencies. So much so, that even core processes such as R&D, manufacturing and marketing are being outsourced today. Haven't you heard of proliferation of 'Business Process Outsourcing' (BPO) and 'Knowledge Process Outsourcing' (KPO)?

(v)   Fulfilling social responsibility: The increased awareness of the public, forces businesses especially limited companies to fulfill their social responsibilities. Management theory and management principles have also evolved in response to these demands. Moreover, the interpretation of the principles also assumes newer and contemporary

———————

meanings with the change in time. So, if one were to talk of 'equity' today, it does not apply to wages alone. Value to the customer, care for the environment, dealings with business associates would all come under the purview of this principle. As an application of this principle, we find that Public Sector Undertakings have developed entire townships as, for example, BHEL has developed Ranipur in Hardwar

(vi)   Management   training,   education   and research:

Principles of management are at the core of management theory. As such these are used as a basis for management training, education and research. You must be aware that entrance to management institutes is preceded by management aptitude tests. Do you think that these tests could have been developed without an understanding of management principles and how they may be applied in different situations? These principles provide basic groundwork for the development of management as a discipline. Professional courses such as MBA (Master of Business Administration), BBA (Bachelor of Business Administration) also teach these principles as part of their curriculum at the beginner's level.

These principles enable refinement of management practices as well by facilitating the development of new management techniques. Thus, we see that techniques like Operations Research (OR), cost accounting, 'Just in Time', 'Kanban' and 'Kaizen' have developed due to further research on these principles.

———————

In conclusion it can be said that understanding the meaning, nature and significance of principles of management will help us to appreciate their applicability in real life situations.

As stated at the beginning of the chapter, management principles have undergone a long history of evolution. And, they continue to evolve. What follows is a description of the management principles pertaining to the classical school; more precisely, those propounded by F.W. Taylor and Henri Fayol.

Taylor's Scientific Management

Scientific management refers to an important stream of one of the earlier schools of thought of management referred to as the 'Classical' school. The other two streams belonging to the classical school are Fayol's Administrative Theory and Max Weber's Bureaucracy. We will not be describing bureaucracy here. A discussion of Fayol's principles, however, will follow the discussion of scientific management.

Fredrick Winslow Taylor (March 20,1856 – March 21, 1915) was an American mechanical engineer who sought to improve industrial efficiency. In 1874, he became an apprentice mechanist, learning factory conditions at the grass roots level. He earned a degree in mechanical engineering. He was one of the intellectual leaders of the efficiency movement and was highly influential in reshaping the factory system of production. You must appreciate that he belonged to the era of the industrial revolution

———————

characterized by mass production. You must also appreciate that every new development takes some time to be perfected. Taylor's contribution must be seen in the light of the efforts made to perfect the factory system of production.

Taylor thought that by scientifically analysing work, it would be possible to find 'one best way' to do it. He is most remembered for his time and motion studies. He would break a job into its component parts and measure each to the second.

Taylor believed that contemporary management was amateurish and should be studied as a discipline. He also wanted that workers should cooperate with the management and thus there would be no need of trade unions. The best results would come from the partnership between a trained and qualified management and a cooperative and innovative workforce. Each side needed the other.

He is known for coinage of the term 'Scientific Management' in his article 'The Principles of Scientific Management' published in 1911. After being fired from Bethlehem Steel Company he wrote a book 'Shop floor' which sold well. He was selected to be the president of the American Society of Mechanical Engineers (ASME) from 1906 to 1907. He was a professor at Tuck School of Business at Dartmouth College founded in 1900.

In 1884 he became an executive at Midvale Steel Company by demonstrating his leadership abilities. He instructed his fellow workers to work in phases. He joined

———————

the Bethlehem Iron Company in 1898, which later became Bethlehem Steel Company. He was originally employed to introduce piece rate wage system. After setting up the wage system, he was given authority and more responsibilities in the company. Using his newfound resources he increased the staff and made Bethlehem a show place for inventive work. Unfortunately, the company was sold to another group and he was discharged.

Principles of Scientific Management

In the earlier days of the Industrial Revolution, in the absence of an established theory of factory organisation, factory owners or managers relied on personal judgment in attending to the problems they confronted in the course of managing their work. This is what is referred to as 'rule of thumb'. Managing factories by rule of thumb enabled them to handle the situations as they arose but suffered from the limitation of a trial and error approach. For their experiences to be emulated, it was important to know what works and why does it work. For this, there was a need to follow an approach that was based on the method of science- defining a problem, developing alternative solutions, anticipating consequences, measuring progress and drawing conclusions.

In this scenario, Taylor emerged as the 'Father of Scientific Management'. He proposed scientific management as opposed to rule of thumb. He broke up human activity into small parts and found out how it could be done effectively, in less time and with increased productivity. It implies conducting business activities according to standardised tools, methods and trained personnel in order to increase the output, improve its quality and reduce costs and wastes.

In the words of Taylor, "Scientific management means knowing exactly what you want men to do and seeing that they do it in the best and cheapest way. The Bethlehem Steel company where Taylor himself worked achieved three-fold increase in productivity by application of scientific management principles. Therefore, it would be in order to discuss these principles.

(i)   Science not Rule of Thumb:

Taylor pioneered the introduction of the method of scientific inquiry into the domain of management practice. We have already referred to the limitations of the rule of thumb approach of management. As different managers would follow their indigenous rules of thumb, it is but a statement of the obvious that all would not be equally effective. Taylor believed that there was only one best method to maximise efficiency. This method can be developed through study and analysis. The method so developed should substitute 'Rule of Thumb' throughout the organisation. Scientific method involved investigation of traditional methods through work-study, unifying the best practices and developing a standard method, which would be followed throughout the organisation. According to Taylor, even a small production activity like loading pigs of

———————

iron into boxcars can be scientifically planned and managed. This can result in tremendous saving of human energy as well as wastage of time and materials. The more sophisticated the processes, greater would be the savings.

In the present context, the use of internet has brought about dramatic improvements in internal efficiencies and customer satisfaction.

(ii)   Harmony, Not Discord:

Factory system of production implied that managers served as a link between the owners and the workers. Since as managers they had the mandate to 'get work done' from the workers, it should not be difficult for you to appreciate that there always existed the possibility of a kind of class-conflict, the mangers versus workers. Taylor recognised that this conflict helped none, the workers, the managers or the factory owners. He emphasised that there should be complete harmony between the management and workers. Both should realise that each one is important. To achieve this state, Taylor called for complete mental revolution on the part of both management and workers. It means that management and workers should transform their thinking. In such a situation even trade unions will not think of going on strike etc.

Management should share the gains of the company, if any, with the workers. At the same time workers should work hard and be willing to embrace change for the good of the company. Both should be part of the family. According to Taylor, 'Scientific management has for its foundation the firm conviction that the true interests of the two are one and the same; that prosperity for the employer cannot exist for a long time unless it is accompanied by prosperity for the employees and vice versa'.

Japanese work culture is a classic example of such a situation. In Japanese companies, paternalistic style of management is in practice. There is complete openness between the management and workers. If at all workers go to strike they wear a black badge but work more than normal working hours to gain the sympathy of the management.

(iii) Cooperation, Not Individualism: There should be complete cooperation between the labour and the management instead of individualism. This principle is an extension of principle of 'Harmony not discord'. Competition should be replaced by cooperation. Both should realise that they need each other.

For this, management should not close its ears to any constructive suggestions made by the employees. They should be rewarded for their suggestions which results in substantial reduction in costs. They should be part of management and, if any important decisions are taken, workers should be taken into confidence.

At the same time workers should desist from going on strike and making unreasonable demands on the management. In fact when there will be open communication system and goodwill there will be no need for even a trade union. Paternalistic style of management, whereby the employer takes care of the needs of employees, would prevail as in the case of Japanese companies.

According to Taylor, there should be an almost equal division of work and responsibility between workers and management. All the day long the management should work almost side by side with the workers helping, encouraging and smoothing the way for them.

(iv) Development of Each and Every Person to His or Her Greatest Efficiency and Prosperity: Industrial efficiency depends to a large extent on personnel competencies. As such, scientific management also stood for worker development. Worker training was essential also to learn the 'best method' developed as a consequence of the scientific approach. Taylor was of the view that the concern for efficiency could be built in right from the process of employee selection. Each person should be scientifically selected. Then work assigned should suit her/his physical, mental and intellectual capabilities. To increase efficiency, they should be given the required training. Efficient employees would produce more and earn more. This will ensure their greatest efficiency and prosperity for both company and workers.

From the foregoing discussion it is clear that Taylor was an ardent supporter of use of scientific method of production in business.

Let us now discuss techniques as specified by him. These are based on the various experiments he conducted during his career.

Techniques of Scientific Management

Functional Foremanship

In the factory system, the foreman represents the managerial figure with whom the workers are in face-to-face contact on a daily basis. In the first chapter of the book, you have seen that the foreman is the lowest ranking manager and the highest ranking worker. He is the pivot around whom revolves the entire production planning, implementation and control. Thus, Taylor concentrated on improving the performance of this role in the factory set-up. In fact, he identified a list of qualities of a good foreman/supervisor and found that no single person could fit them all. This prompted him to suggest functional foremanship through eight persons.

Taylor advocated separation of planning and execution functions. This concept was extended to the lowest level of the shop floor. It was known as functional foremanship. Under the factory manager there was a planning incharge and a production incharge. Under planning incharge four personnel namely instruction card clerk, route clerk, time and cost clerk and a disciplinarian worked. These four personnel would draft instructions for the workers, specify the route of production, prepare time and cost sheet and ensure discipline respectively.

Under Production in charge, personnel who would work were speed boss, gang boss, repair boss, and inspector. These respectively were responsible for timely and accurate completion of job, keeping machines and tools etc., ready for operation by workers, ensure proper working condition of machines and tools and check the quality of work.

Functional foremanship is an extension of the principle of division of work and specialisation to the shop floor. Each worker will have to take orders from these eight foremen in the related process or function of production. Foremen should have intelligence, education, tact, grit, judgment, special knowledge, manual dexterity, and energy, honesty and good health. Since all these qualities could not be found in a single person so Taylor proposed eight specialists. Each specialist is to be assigned work according to her/his qualities. For example, those with technical mastery, intelligence and grit may be given planning work. Those with energy and good health may be assigned execution work.

Standardisation and Simplification of Work

Taylor was an ardent supporter of standardisation. According to him scientific method should be used to analyse methods of production prevalent under the rule of thumb. The best practices can be kept and further refined to develop a standard which should be followed throughout the organisation. This can be done through work-study techniques which include time study, motion study, fatigue study and method study, and which are discussed further in this chapter. It may be pointed out that even the contemporary techniques of business process including reengineering, kaizen (continuous improvement) and benchmarking are aimed at standardising the work.

Standardisation refers to the process of setting standards for every business activity; it can be standardisation of process, raw material, time, product, machinery, methods or working conditions. These standards are the benchmarks, which must be adhered to during production. The objectives of standardisation are:

- Factory Manager
- Production In charge
- Planning In charge
- Instruction Card Clerk
- Time and Cost Clerk
- Route Clerk
- Speed Boss
- Repairs Boss
- Gang Boss
- Inspector
- Disciplinarian
- Workman

(i) To reduce a given line or product to fixed types, sizes and characteristics.

(ii) To establish interchange ability of manufactured parts and products.

(iii) To establish standards of excellence and quality in materials.

———————

(iv) To establish standards of performance of men and machines.

Simplification aims at eliminating superfluous varieties, sizes and dimensions while standardisation implies devising new varieties instead of the existing ones. Simplification aims at eliminating unnecessary diversity of products. It results in savings of cost of labour, machines and tools. It implies reduced inventories, fuller utilisation of equipment and increasing turnover.

Most large companies like Nokia, Toyota and Microsoft etc. have successfully implemented standardisation and simplification. This is evident from their large share in their respective markets.

Method Study

The objective of method study is to find out one best way of doing the job. There are various methods of doing the job. To determine the best way there are several parameters. Right from procurement of raw materials till the final product is delivered to the customer every activity is part of method study. Taylor devised the concept of assembly line by using method study. Ford Motor Company used this concept very successfully. Even now auto companies are using it.

The objective of the whole exercise is to minimise the cost of production and maximise the quality and satisfaction of the customer. For this purpose many techniques like process charts and operations research etc are used.

———————

For designing a car, the assembly line production would entail deciding the sequence of operations, place for men, machines and raw materials etc. All this is part of method study.

Motion Study

Motion study refers to the study of movements like lifting, putting objects, sitting and changing positions etc., which are undertaken while doing a typical job. Unnecessary movements are sought to be eliminated so that it takes less time to complete the job efficiently. For example, Taylor and his associate Frank Gailberth were able to reduce motions in brick layering from 18 to just 5. Taylor demonstrated that productivity increased to about four times by this process.

On close examination of body motions, for example, it is possible to find out:

(i) Motions which are productive

(ii) Motions which are incidental (e.g., going to stores)

(iii) Motions which are unproductive.

Taylor used stopwatches and various symbols and colours to identify different motions. Through motion , Taylor was able to design suitable equipment and tools to educate workers on their use. The results achieved by him were truly remarkable.

Time Study

It determines the standard time taken to perform a well-defined job. Time measuring devices are used for each element of task. The standard time is fixed for the whole of the task by taking several readings. The method of time

_____

study will depend upon volume and frequency of the task, the cycle time of the operation and time measurement costs. The objective of time study is to determine the number of workers to be employed; frame suitable incentive schemes and determine labour costs.

For example, on the basis of several observations it is determined that standard time taken by the worker to make one cardboard box is 20 minutes. So in one hour she/he will make 3 boxes. Assuming that a worker has to put in 8 hours of work in a shift and deducting one hour for rest and lunch, it is determined that in 7 hours a worker makes 21 boxes @ 3 boxes per hour. Now this is the standard task a worker has to do. Wages can be decided accordingly.

Fatigue Study

A person is bound to feel tired physically and mentally if she/he does not rest while working. The rest intervals will help one to regain stamina and work again with the same capacity. This will result in increased productivity. Fatigue study seeks to determine the amount and frequency of rest intervals in completing a task. For example, normally in a plant, work takes place in three shifts of eight hours each. Even in a single shift a worker has to be given some rest interval to take her/his lunch etc. If the work involves heavy manual labour then small pauses have to be frequently given to the worker so that she/he can recharge her/his energy level for optimum contribution.

There can be many causes for fatigue like long working hours, doing unsuitable work, having uncordial relations with the boss or bad working conditions etc. Such hindrances in good performance should be removed.

Differential Piece Wage System

Taylor was a strong advocate of piece wage system. He wanted to differentiate between efficient and inefficient workers. The standard time and other parameters should be determined on the basis of the work-study discussed above. The workers can then be classified as efficient or inefficient on the basis of these standards. He wanted to reward efficient workers. So he introduced different rate of wage payment for those who performed above standard and for those who performed below standard. For example, it is determined that standard output per worker per day is 10 units and those who made standard or more than standard will get Rs. 50 per unit and those below will get Rs. 40 per unit. Now an efficient worker making 11 units will get 11x50= Rs. 550 per day whereas a worker who makes 9 units will get 9×40 = Rs. 360 per day.

According to Taylor, the difference of Rs. 190 should be enough for the inefficient worker to be motivated to perform better. From his own experience, Taylor gives the example of a worker named Schmidt who was able to earn 60% more wages from $1.15 to $1.85 on increasing pig iron loading from 12.5 tons per man per day to 47 tons per man per day in box cars at Bethlehem Steel works by following scientific management techniques.

It is important to have a relook at the techniques of scientific management as comprising a unified whole of

Taylor's prescription of efficiency. Search for efficiency requires the search for one best method and the chosen method must lead to the determination of a fair day's work. There must be a compensation system that differentiates those who are able to accomplish/exceed the fair day's work. This differential system must be based on the premise that efficiency is the result of the joint efforts of the managers and the workers. Thus, rather than quarrelling over the share in the resultant surplus, the workers and managers should work in harmony for maximising the output rather than restricting it. Clearly the sum and substance of Taylor's ideas lies not in the disjointed description of principles and techniques of scientific management, but in the change of the mindset, which he referred to as mental revolution. Mental revolution involves a change in the attitude of workers and management towards one another from competition to cooperation. Both should realise that they require one another. Both should aim to increase the size of surplus. This would eliminate the need for any agitation. Management should share a part of surplus with workers. Workers should also contribute their might so that the company makes profits. This attitude will be good for both of them and also for the company. In the long run only worker's well-being will ensure prosperity of the business.

Now, having studied the elements, principles and techniques of scientific management we can consider the practical applications of the same at the time of F.W. Taylor and in the present.

———————

We can also examine the present status of scientific management. Today, many new techniques have been developed as a sequel to scientific management. Operations research was developed in the second World War to optimise the deployment of war material. Similarly assembly line was also discovered by F.W. Taylor, which was used very successfully by Ford motor company for manufacturing 'Model T' car for the masses. This concept is much used now. The latest development in scientific management is 'LEAN MANUFACTURING'. Now a days robotics and computers are being used in production and other business activities. This is part of scientific management of these activities. It has increased productivity levels. The techniques of operation research have also been developed and are being used as a result of scientific management. The box below gives meanings of some terms used in modern manufacturing.

Fayol's Principles of Management

In the development of classical school of management thought, Fayol's administrative theory provides an important link. While Taylor succeeded in revolutionizing the working of factory shop-floor in terms of devising the best method, fair day's work, differential piece-rate system and functional foremanship; Henri Fayol explained what amounts to a managers work and what principles should be followed in doing this work. If workers' efficiency mattered in the factory system, so does the managerial efficiency. Fayol's contribution must be interpreted in terms of the impact that his writings had and continue to have improvement in managerial efficiencies.

Henri Fayol (1841-1925) was a French management theorist whose theories concerning scientific organisation of labour were widely influential in the beginning of twentieth century. He graduated from the mining academy of St. Etienne in 1860 in mining engineering. The 19 year old engineer started at the mining company 'Companies de commentary-Fourchambean-Decazeville, ultimately acting as its managing director from 1888 to 1918.

His theories deal with organisation of production in the context of a competitive enterprise that has to control its production costs. Fayol was the first to identify four functions of management – Planning, Organising, Directing and Controlling although his version was a bit different – Plan, Organise, Command, Coordinate and Control. According to Fayol, all activities of an industrial undertaking could be divided into: Technical; Commercial; Financial; Security; Accounting and Managerial. He also suggested that qualities a manager must possess should be — Physical, Moral, Education, Knowledge and experience. He believed that the number of management principles that might help to improve an organisation's operation is potentially limitless.

Based largely on his own experience, he developed his concept of administration. The 14 principles of management propounded by him were discussed in detail in his book published in 1917, 'Administration industrielle et generale'.

———————

It was published in English as 'General and Industrial Management' in 1949 and is widely considered a foundational work in classical management theory. For his contribution he is also known as the 'Father of General Management'

The 14 principles of management given by him are:

(i) **Division of Work:** Work is divided into small tasks/jobs. A trained specialist who is competent is required to perform each job. Thus, division of work leads to specialisation. According to Fayol, "The intent of division of work is to produce more and better work for the same effort. Specialisation is the most efficient way to use human effort."

In business work can be performed more efficiently if it is divided into specialised tasks; each performed by a specialist or trained employee. This results in efficient and effective output. Thus, in a company we have separate departments for finance, marketing, production 19 year old engineer started at the mining company 'Compagnie de commentary-Fourchambean-Decazeville, ultimately acting as its managing director from 1888 to 1918.

His theories deal with organisation of production in the context of a competitive enterprise that has to control its production costs. Fayol was the first to identify four functions of management – Planning, Organising, Directing and Controlling although his version was a bit different – Plan, Organise, Command, Coordinate and Control. According to Fayol, all activities of an industrial undertaking

————————

could be divided into: Technical; Commercial; Financial; Security; Accounting and Managerial. He also suggested that qualities a manager must possess should be — Physical, Moral, Education, Knowledge and experience. He believed that the number of management principles that might help to improve an organisation's operation is potentially limitless.

Based largely on his own experience, he developed his concept of administration. The 14 principles of management propounded by him were discussed in detail in his book published in 1917, 'Administration industrielle et generale'. It was published in English as 'General and Industrial Management' in 1949 and is widely considered a foundational work in classical management theory. For his contribution he is also known as the 'Father of General Management'

The 14 principles of management given by him are:

(i) **Division of Work:** Work is divided into small tasks/jobs. A trained specialist who is competent is required to perform each job. Thus, division of work leads to specialisation. According to Fayol, "The intent of division of work is to produce more and better work for the same effort. Specialisation is the most efficient way to use human effort."

In business work can be performed more efficiently if it is divided into specialised tasks; each performed by a specialist or trained employee. This results in efficient and effective output. Thus, in a company we have separate departments for finance, marketing, production and human resource development etc. All of them have specialised persons. Collectively they achieve production and sales targets of the company. Fayol applies this principle of division of work to all kinds of work — technical as well as managerial. You can observe this principle at work in any organisation like hospital or even a government office.

(ii) **Authority and Responsibility:** According to Fayol, "Authority is the right to give orders and obtain obedience, and responsibility is the corollary of authority. The two types of authority are official authority, which is the authority to command, and personal authority which is the authority of the individual manager."

Authority is both formal and informal. Managers require authority commensurate with their responsibility. There should be a balance between authority and responsibility. An organisation should build safeguards against abuse of managerial power. At the same time a manager should have necessary authority to carry out his responsibility. For example, a sales manager has to negotiate a deal with a buyer. She finds that if she can offer credit period of 60 days she is likely to clinch the deal which is supposed to fetch the company net margin of say Rs. 50 crores. Now the company gives power to the manager to offer a credit period of only 40 days. This shows that there is an imbalance in authority and responsibility. In this case the manager should be granted authority of offering credit period of 60 days in the interest of the company. Similarly, in

————————

this example this manager should not be given a power to offer a credit period of say 100 days because it is not required. A manager should have the right to punish a subordinate for willfully not obeying a legitimate order but only after sufficient opportunity has been given to a subordinate for presenting her/his case.

(iii) **Discipline:** Discipline is the obedience to organisational rules and employment agreement which are necessary for the working of the organisation. According to Fayol, discipline requires good superiors at all levels, clear and fair agreements and judicious application of penalties.

Suppose management and labour union have entered into an agreement whereby workers have agreed to put in extra hours without any additional payment to revive the company out of loss. In return the management has promised to increase wages of the workers when this mission is accomplished. Here discipline when applied would mean that the workers and management both honour their commitments without any prejudice towards one another.

(iv) **Unity of Command:** According to Fayol there should be one and only one boss for every individual employee. If an employee gets orders from two superiors at the same time the principle of unity of command is violated. The principle of unity of command states that each participant in a formal organisation should receive orders from and be responsible to only one superior. Fayol gave a lot of importance to this principle. He felt that if this principle is violated "authority is undermined, discipline is in

_____

jeopardy, order disturbed and stability threatened". The principle resembles military organisation. Dual subordination should be avoided. This is to prevent confusion regarding tasks to be done. Suppose a sales person is asked to clinch a deal with a buyer and is allowed to give 10% discount by the marketing manager. But finance department tells her/him not to offer more than 5% discount. Now there is no unity of command. This can be avoided if there is coordination between various departments.

(v) **Unity of Direction:** All the units of an organisation should be moving towards the same objectives through coordinated 58 Business Studies and focussed efforts. Each group of activities having the same objective must have one head and one plan. This ensures unity of action and coordination. For example, if a company is manufacturing motorcycles as well as cars then it should have two separate divisions for both of them. Each division should have its own incharge, plans and execution resources. On no account should the working of two divisions overlap. Now let us differentiate between the two principles of unity of command and unity of direction.

(vi) **Subordination of Individual Interest to General Interest:** The interests of an organisation should take priority over the interests of any one individual employee according to Fayol. Every worker has some individual interest for working in a company. The company has got its own objectives. For example, the company would want to get maximum output from its employees at a competitive cost

———————

(salary). On the other hand, an employee may want to get maximum salary while working the least. In another situation an individual employee may demand some concession, which is not admissible to any other employee like working for less time.

In all the situations the interests of the group/company will supersede the interest of any one individual. This is so because larger interests of the workers and stakeholders are more important than the interest of any one person. For example, interests of various stakeholders i.e., owners, shareholders, creditors, debtors, financers, tax authorities, customers and the society at large cannot be sacrificed for one individual or a small group of individuals who want to exert pressure on the company. A manager can ensure this by her/his exemplary behaviour. For example, she/he should not fall into temptation of misusing her/his powers for individual/ family benefit at the cost of larger general interest of the workers/ company. This will raise her/his stature in the eyes of the workers and at the same time ensure same behaviour by them.

(vii) Remuneration of Employees: The overall pay and compensation should be fair to both employees and the organisation. The employees should be paid fair wages, which should give them at least a reasonable standard of living. At the same time it should be within the paying capacity of the company. In other words, remuneration should be just and equitable. This will ensure congenial atmosphere and good relations between workers and

_____

management. Consequently, the working of the company would be smooth.

(viii) Centralisation and Decentralisation: The concentration of decision-making authority is called centralisation whereas its dispersal among more than one person is known as decentralisation. According to Fayol, "There is a need to balance subordinate involvement through decentralisation with managers' retention of final authority through centralisation." The degree of centralisation will depend upon the circumstances in which the company is working. In general large organisations have more decentralisation than small organisations. For example, panchayats in our country have been given more powers to decide and spend funds granted to them by the government for the welfare of villages. This is decentralisation at the national level.

(ix) Scalar Chain: An organisation consists of superiors and subordinates. The formal lines of authority from highest to lowest ranks are known as scalar chain.

According to Fayol, "Organisa-tions should have a chain of authority and communication that runs from top to bottom and should be followed by managers and the subordinates."

Let us consider a situation where there is one head 'A' who has two lines of authority under her/him. One line consists of B-C-D-E-F. Another line of authority under 'A' is L-M-N-O-P. If 'E' has to communicate with 'O' who is at the same level of authority then she/he has to traverse the route

E-D-C-B-A-L-M-N-O. This is due to the principle of scalar chain being followed in this situation. According to Fayol, this chain should not be violated in the normal course of formal communication. However, if there is an emergency then 'E' can directly contact 'O' through 'Gang Plank' as shown in the diagram. This is a shorter route and has been provided so that communication is not delayed. In practice you find that a worker cannot directly contact the CEO of the company. If at all she/he has to, then all the formal levels i.e., foreman, superintendent, manager, director etc have to know about the matter. However, in an emergency it can be possible that a worker can contact CEO directly.

(x) Order: According to Fayol, "People and materials must be in suitable places at appropriate time for maximum efficiency." The principle of order states that 'A place for everything (everyone) and everything (everyone) in its (her/his) place'. Essentially it means orderliness. If there is a fixed place for everything and it is present there, then there will be no hindrance in the activities of business/ factory. This will lead to increased productivity and efficiency.

(xi) Equity: Good sense and experience are needed to ensure fairness to all employees, who should be treated as fairly as possible," according to Fayol. This principle emphasises kindliness and justice in the behaviour of managers towards workers. This will ensure loyalty and devotion. Fayol does not rule out use of force sometimes. Rather he says that lazy personnel should be dealt with sternly to send the message that everyone is equal in the eyes of the management. There should be no discrimination against anyone on account of sex, religion, language, caste, belief or nationality etc. In practice we can observe that now a days in multinational corporations people of various nationalities work together in a discrimination free environment.

Fayol's Scalar Chain

Equal opportunities are available for everyone in such companies to rise. Thus, we find India-born CEO's such as Rajat Gupta who heads multinational like Mckinsey Inc. Lately India-born American Arun Sarin has become CEO of Vodaphone limited, a British telecom major.

(xii) Stability of Personnel: "Employee turnover should be minimised to maintain organisational efficiency", according to Fayol. Personnel should be selected and appointed after due and rigorous procedure. But once selected they should be kept at their post/position for a minimum fixed tenure. They should have stability of tenure. They should be given reasonable time to show results. Any adhocism in this regard will create instability/insecurity among employees. They would tend to leave the organisation. Recruitment, selection and training cost will be high. So stability in tenure of personnel is good for the business.

(xiii) Initiative: Workers should be encouraged to develop and carry out their plans for improvements according to Fayol. Initiative means taking the first step with self-motivation. It is thinking out and executing the plan. It is

———————

one of the traits of an intelligent person. Initiative should be encouraged. But it does not mean going against the established practices of the company for the sake of being different. A good company should have an employee suggestion system whereby initiative/suggestions which result in substantial cost/time reduction should be rewarded.

(xiv) Espirit De Corps: Management should promote a team spirit of unity and harmony among employees, according to Fayol. Management should promote teamwork especially in large organisations because otherwise objectives would be difficult to realise. It will also result in a loss of coordination. A manager should replace 'I' with 'We' in all his conversations with workers to foster team spirit. This will give rise to a spirit of mutual trust and belongingness among team members. It will also minimise the need for using penalties.

From the foregoing discussion it is clear that Fayol's 14 principles of management are widely applicable to managerial problems and have cast a profound impact on management thinking today. But with the change of environment in which business is done, the interpretation of these principles has changed. For example, authority and responsibility meant empowering of managers but now it means empowerment of employees because of flat organisational structures that are gaining ground. We are now in a position to understand the current connotations of Fayol's principles discussed in the accompanying box.

Fayol Versus Taylor — A Comparison

———————

We are now in a position to compare the contributions of both Fayol and Taylor. Both of them have contributed immensely to the knowledge of management, which has formed a basis for further practice by managers. It must be pointed out that their contributions are complementary to each other. We can make out the following points of difference between their contributions.

You may also like to have some knowledge of contributions of Indians to the growth of management knowledge training cost will be high. So stability in tenure of personnel is good for the business.

Sl. No.	Basis of difference	Henri Fayol	F. W. Taylor
1.	Perspective	Top level of management	Shop floor level of a factory
2.	Unity of Command	Staunch Proponent	Did not feel that it is important as under functional foremanship a worker received orders from eight specialists.
.	Applicability	Applicable universally	Applicable to specialised situations
.	Basis of formation	Personal experience	Observations and experimentation
.	Focus	Improving overall administration	Increasing Productivity
	Personality	Practitioner	Scientist

———————————

.			
.	Expression	General Theory of Administration	Scientific Management

BUSINESS ENVIRONMENT

Meaning of Business Environment

The term 'business environment' means the sum total of all individuals, institutions and other forces that are outside the control of a business enterprise but that may affect its performance. As one writer has put it– "Just take the universe, subtract from it the subset that represents the organisation, and the remainder is environment". Thus, the economic, social, political, technological and other forces which operate outside a business enterprise are part of its environment. So also, the individual consumers or competing enterprises as well as the governments, consumer groups, competitors, courts, media and other institutions working outside an enterprise constitute its environment. The important point is that these individuals, institutions and forces are likely to influence the performance of a business enterprise although they happen to exist outside its boundaries. For example, changes in government's economic policies, rapid technological developments, political uncertainty, changes in fashions and tastes of consumers and increased competition in the market — all influence the working of a business enterprise in important ways. Increase in taxes by government can make things expensive to buy. Technological improvements may render existing products obsolete. Political uncertainty may create fear in the minds of investors. Changes in fashions and tastes of consumers may shift demand in the market from existing products to new ones. Increased competition in the market may reduce profit margins of firms.

On the basis of the foregoing discussion, it can be said business environment, has the following features:

(i) Totality of external forces: Business environment is the sum total of all things external to business firms and, as such, is aggregative in nature.

(ii) Specific and general forces: Business environment includes both specific and general forces. Specific forces (such as investors, customers, competitors and suppliers) affect individual enterprises directly and immediately in their day-to-day working. General forces (such as social, political, legal and technological conditions) have impact on all business enterprises and thus may affect an individual firm only indirectly.

(iii) Inter-relatedness: Different elements or parts of business environment are closely inter-related. For example, increased life expectancy of people and increased awareness for health care have increased the demand for many health products and services like diet Coke, fat-free cooking oil, and health resorts. New health products and services have, in turn, changed people's life styles.

(iv) Dynamic nature: Business environment is dynamic in that it keeps on changing whether in terms of technological

———————

improvement, shifts in consumer preferences or entry of new competition in the market.

(v) Uncertainty: Business environment is largely uncertain as it is very difficult to predict future happenings, especially when environment changes are taking place too frequently as in the case of information technology or fashion industries.

(vi) Complexity: Since business environment consists of numerous interrelated and dynamic cond-itions or forces which arise from different sources, it becomes difficult to comprehend at once what exactly constitutes a given environment. In other words, environment is a complex phenomenon that is relatively easier to understand in parts but difficult to grasp in its totality. For example, it may be difficult to know the extent of the relative impact of the social, economic, political, technological or legal factors on change in demand of a product in the market.

(vii) Relativity: Business environment is a relative concept since it differs from country to country and even region to region. Political conditions in the USA, for instance, differ from those in China or Pakistan. Similarly, demand for sarees may be fairly high in India whereas it may be almost non-existent in France.

Importance of Business Environment

Just like human beings, business enterprises do not exist in isolation. Each business firm is not an island unto itself; it exists, survives and grows within the context of the element and forces of its environment. While an individual firm is able to do little to change or control these forces, it has no alternative to responding or adapting according to them. A good understanding of environment by business managers enables them not only to identify and evaluate, but also to react to the forces external to their firms. The importance of business environment and its understanding by managers can be appreciated if we consider the following facts:

(i) It enables the firm to identify opportunities and getting the first mover advantage: Opportunities refer to the positive external trends or changes that will help a firm to improve its performance. Environment provides numerous opportunities for business success. Early identification of opportunities helps an enterprise to be the first to exploit them instead of losing them to competitors. For example, Maruti Udyog became the leader in the small car market because it was the first to recognise the need for small cars in an environment of rising petroleum prices and a large middle class population in India.

(ii) It helps the firm to identify threats and early warning signals: Threats refer to the external environment trends and changes that will hinder a firm's performance. Besides opportunities, environment happens to be the source of many threats. Environmental awareness can help managers to identify various threats on time and serve as an early warning signal. For example, if an Indian firm finds that a foreign multinational is entering the Indian market with new substitutes, it should act as a warning signal. On the basis of this information, the Indian firms can prepare themselves to meet the threat by adopting such measures as improving the quality of the product, reducing cost of the production, engaging in aggressive advertising, and so on.

(iii) It helps in tapping useful resources: Environment is a source of various resources for running a business. To engage in any type of activity, a business enterprise assembles various resources called inputs like finance, machines, raw materials, power and water, labour, etc., from its environment including financiers, government and suppliers. They decide to provide these resources with their own expectations to get something in return from the enterprise. The business enterprise supplies the environment with its outputs such as goods and services for customers, payment of taxes to government, return on financial investment to investors and so on. Because the enterprise depends on the environment as a source of inputs or resources and as an outlet for outputs, it only makes sense that the enterprise designs policies that allow it to get the resources that it needs so that it can convert those resources into outputs that the environment desires. This can be done better by understanding what the environment has to offer.

(iv) It helps in coping with rapid changes: Today's business environment is getting increasingly dynamic where changes are taking place at a fast pace. It is not the fact of change itself that is so important as the pace of change. Turbulent market conditions, less brand loyalty, divisions and sub-divisions (fragmentation) of markets, more demanding customers, rapid changes in technology and intense global competition are just a few of the images used to describe today's business environment. All sizes and all types of enterprises are facing increasingly dynamic environment. In order to effectively cope with these significant changes, managers must understand and examine the environment and develop suitable courses of action.

(v) It helps in assisting in planning and policy formulation: Since environment is a source of both opportunities and threats for a business enterprise, its understanding and analysis can be the basis for deciding the future course of action (planning) or training guidelines for decision making (policy). For instance, entry of new players in the market, which means more competition may make an enterprise think afresh about how to deal with the situation.

(vi) It helps in improving performance: The final reason for understanding business environment relates to whether or not it really makes a difference in the performance of an enterprise. The answer is that it does appear to make a difference. Many studies reveal that the future of an enterprise is closely bound up with what is happening in the environment. And, the enterprises that continuously monitor their environment and adopt suitable business practices are the ones which not only improve their present performance but also continue to succeed in the market for a longer period.

Dimensions of Business Environment

———————

Dimensions of, or the factors constituting the business environment include economic, social, technological, political and legal conditions which are considered relevant for decision-making and improving the performance of an enterprise. In contrast to the specific environment, these factors explain the general environment which mostly influences many enterprises at the same time. However, management of every enterprise can benefit from being aware of these dimensions instead of being disinterested in them. For instance, scientific research has discovered a technology that makes it possible to produce an energy efficient light bulb that lasts at least twenty times as long as a standard bulb. Senior managers in the lighting divisions at General Electric and Phillips recognised that this discovery had the potential to significantly affect their unit growth and profitability, So they have carefully followed the progress on this research and profitably used its findings.

Discussion of the various factors constituting the general environment of business is given below:

(i) Economic Environment: Interest rates, inflation rates, changes in disposable income of people, stock market indices and the value of rupee are some of the economic factors that can affect management practices in a business enterprise. Short and long term interest rates significantly affect the demand for product and services. For example, in case of construction companies and automobile manufacturers, low longer-term rates are beneficial because they result in increased spending by consumers for buying homes and cars on borrowed money. Similarly, a rise in the disposable income of people due to increase in the gross domestic product of a country creates increasing demand for products. High inflation rates generally result in constraints on business enterprises as they increase the various costs of business such as the purchase of raw materials or machinery and payment of wages and salaries to employees. And non-discriminatory employment practices. Social trends present various opportunities and threats to business enterprises. For example, the health-and-fitness trend has become popular among large number of urban dwellers. This has created a demand for products like organic food, diet soft drinks, gyms, bottled (mineral) water and food supplements. This trend has, however, harmed business in other industries like dairy processing, tobacco and liquor.

(iii) Technological Environment: Technological environment includes forces relating to scientific improvements and innovations which provide new ways of producing goods and services and new methods and techniques of operating a business. For example, recent technological, advances in computers and electronics have modified the ways in

(ii) Social Environment: The social environment of business include the social forces like customs and traditions, values, social trends, society's expectations from business, etc. Traditions define social practices that have lasted for decades or even centuries. For example, the celebration of Diwali, Id, Christmas, and Guru Parv in India provides significant financial opportunities for greetings card

——————

companies, sweets or confectionery manufacturers, tailoring outlets and many other related business. Values refer to concepts that a society holds in high esteem. In India, individual freedom, social justice, equality of opportunity and national integration are examples of major values cherished by all of us. In business terms, these values translate into freedom of choice in the market, business's responsibility towards the society

- Attitudes towards product innovations, lifestyles, occupational distribution and consumer preferences
- Concern with quality of life
- Life expectancy
- Expectations from the workforce
- Shifts in the presence of women in the workforce
- Birth and death rates
- Population shifts
- Educational system and literacy rates
- Consumption habits
- Composition of family

Major Elements of Social Environment

SOCIAL ENVIRONMENT

Contact any ten families known to you. Find out the changes in their consumption habits over the last five years. Analyse the impact of these changes on the working of business enterprises.

Impact of shifts with the presence of women in the workforce Because of technological advancement, it has

---

become possible to book railway tickets through Internet from home, office etc..

Indian Railway Catering and Tourism Corporation ltd.
(A Government of India Enterprise)
E-TICKET BOOKING ON THIS WEBSITE - A GUIDE

- Register as an individual. Registration is FREE.
- Login by entering your user name and password.
- The 'Plan my travel and Book tickets' page appears.
- Use 'HELP' option for any help required to book tickets.
- Fill in the details, by following the guidelines given below.

which companies advertise their products. It is common now to see CD-ROM's, computerised information kiosks, and Internet/ World Wide Web multimedia pages highlighting the virtues of products. Similarly, retailers have direct links with suppliers who replenish stocks when needed. Manufacturers have flexible manufacturing systems. Airline companies have Internet and World Wide Web pages where customers can look for flight times, destinations and fares and book their tickets online. In addition, continuing innovations in different scientific and engineering fields such as lasers, robotics, biotechnology, food preservatives, medicine, telecommunication and synthetic fuels have provided numerous opportunities and threats for many different enterprises. Shifts in demand from vaccum tubes to transistors, from steam locomotives to dieseland electric

———————

engines, from fountain pens to ballpoint, from propeller airplanes to jets, and from typewriters to computer based word processors, have all been responsible and creating new business.

(iv) Political Environment: Political environment includes political conditions such as general stability and peace in the country and specific attitudes that elected government representatives hold towards business. The significance of political conditions in business success lies in the predictability of business activities under stable political conditions. On the other hand, there may be uncertainty of business activities due to political unrest and threats to law and order. Political stability,

- The Constitution of the country
- Prevailing political system
- The degree of politicization of business and economic issues
- Dominant ideologies and values of major political parties
- The nature and profile of political leadership and thinking of political personalities
- The level of political morality
- Political institutions like the government and allied agencies
- Political ideology and practices of the ruling party
- The extent and nature of government intervention in business

---

- The nature of relationship of our country with foreign countries

Major Elements of Political Environment

thus, builds up confidence among business people to invest in the long term projects for the growth of the economy. Political instability can shake that confidence. Similarly, the attitudes of government officials towards business may have either positive or negative impact upon business. For example, even after opening up of our economy in 1991, foreign companies found it extremely difficult to cut through the bureaucratic red tape to get permits for doing business in India. Sometimes, it took months to process even their application for the purpose. As a result these companies were discouraged from investing in our country. The situation has improved over time.

(v) Legal Environment: Legal environment includes various legislations passed by the Government administrative orders issued by government authorities, court judgments as well as the decisions rendered by various commissions and agencies at every level of the government— centre, state or local. It is imperative for the management of every enterprise to obey the law of the land. Therefore, an adequate knowledge of rules and regulations framed by the Government is a pre-requisite for better business performance. Non-compliance of laws can land the business enterprise into legal problems. In India, a working knowledge of Companies Act 1956; Industries (Development and Regulations) Act 1951; Foreign

———————

Exchange Management Act and the Imports and Exports (Control) Act 1947; Factories Act, 1948; Trade Union Act; 1926; Workmen's Compensation Act, 1923; Industrial Disputes Act, 1947, Consumer Protection Act, 1986, Competition Act, 2002 and host of such other legal enactments as amended from time to time by the Parliament, is important for doing business. Impact of legal environment can be illustrated with the help of government regulations to protect consumer's interests. For example, the advertisement of alcoholic beverages is prohibited. Advertisements, including packets of cigarettes carry the statutory warning 'Cigarette smoking is injurious to health'. Similarly, advertisements of baby food must necessarily inform the potential buyer that mothers milk is the best. All these regulations are required to be followed by advertisers.

Economic Environment in India

The economic environment in India consists of various macro-level factors

related to the means of production and distribution of wealth which have an impact on business and industry. These include:

(a) Stage of economic development of the country.

(b) The economic structure in the form of mixed economy which recognises the role of both public and private sectors.

(c) Economic policies of the Government, including industrial, monetary and fiscal policies.

(d) Economic planning, including five year plans, annual budgets, and so on.

(e) Economic indices, like national income, distribution of income, rate and growth of GNP, per capita income, disposal personal income, rate of savings and investments, value of exports and imports, balance of payments, and so on.

(f) Infrastructural factors, such as, financial institutions, banks, modes of transportation communication facilities, and so on. Business enterprises in India do realize the importance and impact of the economic environment on their working. Almost all annual company reports presented by their chairpersons devote considerable attention to the general economic environment prevailing in the country and an assessment of its impact on their companies.

The economic environment of business in India has been steadily changing mainly due to the government policies. At the time of Independence:

(a) The Indian economy was mainly agricultural and rural in character;

(b) About 70% of the working population
was employed in agriculture;

(c) About 85% of the population was living in the villages;

(d) Production was carried out using irrational, low productivity technology;

(e) Communicable diseases were widespread, mortality rates were high. These was no good public health system.

In order to solve economic problems of our country, the government took several steps including control by the State of certain industries, central planning and reduced

———————

importance of the private sector. The main objectives of India's development plans were:

(a) Initiate rapid economic growth to raise the standard of living, reduce unemployment and poverty;

(b) Become self-reliant and set up a strong industrial base with emphasis on heavy and basic industries;

(c) Reduce inequalities of income and wealth;

(d) Adopt a socialist pattern of development — based on equality and prevent exploitation of man by man.

In accordance with the economic planning, the government gave a lead role to the public sector for

Major elements of the crisis situation which led the **Government of India to announce economic reform were:**

- A serious fiscal crisis in which the fiscal deficit reached the level of 6.6 per cent of GDP in 1990-91.

- Heavy internal debt which rose to about 50 per cent of GDP with interest payments draining about 39 per cent of total revenue collections of the central government.

- Low GNP growth rate which fell to 1.4 per cent from the peak level of 10.5 per cent in 1988-89 (at 1980-81 prices).

- Low overall agricultural production, food grain production and industrial production showed negative growth rates of –2.8 per cent, –5.3 per cent and –0.1 per cent respectively.

_____

- Soaring inflation rate based both on wholesale price index and consumer price index (for industrial workers) at 13-14 per cent.
- Shrinkage of foreign trade, imports (in $ terms) fell by 19.4 per cent and exports by 1.5 per cent.
- Depreciation of rupee by 26.7 per cent vis-à-vis US dollars.
- Fall of foreign exchange reserves to such a low level that they were barely adequate to meet the import requirements of a few weeks.
- Non-resident Indians (NRIs) were withdrawing their deposits at an alarmingly high rate.
- The confidence of the international financial institutions was badly shaken and in just over a year its creditworthiness rating fell from AAA to BB+ (put on credit watch).
- The country was on the verge of defaulting on international financial obligations and the situation warranted immediate policy action to save the situation. In May 1991, the Government had to lease 20 tones of gold out of its stock to the State Bank of India to enable it to sell the gold with repurchase option after six months. In addition, Reserve Bank of India was allowed to pledge 47 tones of gold to the Bank of England to raise a loan of $600 million.

Crisis of June 1991 infrastructure industries whereas the private sector was broadly given the responsibility of developing consumer goods industry. At the same time, the

―――――――――

government imposed several restrictions, regulations and controls on the working of private sector enterprises. India's experience with economic planning has delivered mixed results. In 1991 the economy faced a serious foreign exchange crisis, high government deficit and a rising trend of prices despite bumper crops.

As a part of economic reforms, the Government of India announced a new industrial policy in July 1991.

The broad features of this policy were as follows:

(a) The Government reduced the number of industries under compulsory licensing to six.

(b) Many of the industries reserved for the public sector under the earlier policy, were dereserved. The role of the public sector was limited only to four industries of strategic importance.

(c) Disinvestment was carried out in case of many public sector industrial enterprises.

(d) Policy towards foreign capital was liberalised. The share of foreign equity participation was increased and in many activities 100 per cent Foreign Direct Investment (FDI) was permitted.

(e) Automatic permission was now granted for technology agreements with foreign companies.

(f) Foreign Investment Promotion Board (FIPB) was set up to promote and channelise foreign investment in India.

Appropriate measures were taken to remove obstacles in the way of growth and expansion of industrial units of large

_____

industrial houses. Small-scale sector was assured all help and accorded due recognition.

In essence, this policy has sought to liberate industry from the shackles of the licensing system (liberalisation), drastically reduce the role of the public sector (privatisation) and encourage foreign private participation in India's industrial development (globalisation).

Liberalisation: The economic reforms that were introduced were aimed at liberalising the Indian business and industry from all unnecessary controls and restrictions. They signalled the end of the licence-pemit-quota raj. Liberalisation of the Indian industry has taken place with respect to:

(i) abolishing licensing requirement in most of the industries except a short list,

(ii) freedom in deciding the scale of business activities i.e., no restrictions on expansion or contraction of business activities,

(iii) removal of restrictions on the movement of goods and services,

(iv) freedom in fixing the prices of goods services,

(v) reduction in tax rates and lifting of unnecessary controls over the economy,

(vi) simplifying procedures for imports and experts, and

(vii) making it easier to attract foreign capital and technology to India.

Privatisation: The new set of economic reforms aimed at giving greater role to the private sector in the nation building process and a reduced role to the public sector. This was a

———————————

reversal Some of the early major steps taken to manage the economic crisis were the following:

of the Central Government by large companies for capacity expansion, diversification and merger and amalgamation.

- Nine areas in basic and core industries earlier reserved for the public sector were opened to the private sector;
- Limit of foreign equity holding raised from 40 per cent to 51 per cent in a wide range of priority industries;
- Foreign Investment Promotion Board (FIPB) established to negotiate proposals from large international firms and expedite clearances of the investment proposals;
- Rupee devaluation by 18 per cent during July 1-3, 1991 supported by a standby credit of $2.3 billion from the IMP over a 20 months period negotiated in October 1991;
- Negotiation of $500 million Structural Adjustment Loan from the World Bank in April 1992 and a loan totalling SDR 1.3 billion from the International Monetory Fund (IMF) between January-September 1991;
- Introduction of India Development Bond Scheme and Immunity Scheme for repatriation of funds held abroad in October 1991, under which more than $2 billion were mobilised during 1991-92;
- Bringing back of gold earlier pledged to the Bank of England and the Bank of Japan;

———————

- Continuance of the measures of import control and credit squeeze;
- Administered licensing of imports replaced by freely tradeable import entitlements (called Eximscrips) linked to export earnings. The measure was expected to introduce self-balancing mechanism in India's foreign trade;
- Introduction of Liberalised Exchange Rate Management System (LERMS) under which a dual exchange rate system was established, one rate being effectively floated in the market; and
- Import licensing in most capital goods, raw materials, intermediates and components eliminated. Advance Licensing System considerably simplified.

The initial series of measures set the tone for the future economic reforms. Any of the measures taken above was continued to form a part of the ongoing reform process.

Early Crisis Met : Reform Measures of the development strategy pursued so far by Indian planners. To achieve this, the government redefined the role of the public sector in the New Industrial Policy of 1991, adopted the policy of planned disinvestments of the public sector and decided to refer the loss making and sick enterprises to the Board of Industrial and Financial Reconstruction. The term disinvestments used here means transfer in the public sector enterprises to the private sector. It results in dilution of stake of the Government in the public enterprise. If there is dilution of Government ownership beyond 51 percent, it would result in

_____

transfer of ownership and management of the enterprise to the private sector.

Globalisation: Globalisation means the integration of the various economies of the world leading towards the emergence of a cohesive global economy. Till 1991, the Government of India had followed a policy of strictly regulating imports in value and volume terms. These regulations were with respect to (a) licensing of imports, (b) tariff restrictions and (c) quantitative restrictions. The new economic reforms aimed at trade liberalisation were directed towards import liberalisation, export promotion through rationalisation of the tariff structure and reforms with respect to foreign exchange so that the country does not remain isolated from the rest of the world. Globalisation involves an increased level of interaction and interdependence among the various nations of the global economy.

Physical geographical gap or political

A truly global economy implies a boundaryless world where there is:

(i) Free flow of goods and services across nations;

(ii) Free flow of capital across nations;

(iii) Free flow of information and technology;

(iv) Free movement of people across borders;

(v)A common acceptable mechanism for the settlement of disputes;

(vi) A global governance perspective.

———————

boundaries no longer remain barriers for a business enterprise to serve a customer in a distant geographical market. This has been made possible by the rapid advancement in technology and liberal trade policies by Governments. Through the policy of 1991, the government of India moved the country to this globalisation pattern.

Impact of Government Policy Changes on Business and Industry

The policy of liberalisation, privatisation and globalisation of the Government has made a significant impact on the working of enterprises in business and industry. The Indian corporate sector has come face-to-face with several challenges due to government policy changes. These challenges can be explained as follows:

(i) Increasing competition: As a result of changes in the rules of industrial licensing and entry of foreign firms, competition for Indian firms has increased especially in service industries like telecommunications, airlines, banking, insurance, etc. which were earlier in the public sector.

(ii) More demanding customers: Customers today have become more demanding because they are well-informed. Increased competition in the market gives the customers wider choice in purchasing better quality of goods and services.

(iii) Repidly changing technological environment: Increased competition forces the firms to develop new ways to survive and grow in the market. New technologies make

———————

it possible to improve machines, process, products and services. The rapidly changing technological environment creates tough challenges before smaller firms.

(iv) Necessity for change: In a regulated environment of pre-1991 era, the firms could have relatively stable policies and practices. After 1991, the market forces have become turbulent as a result of which the enterprises have to continuously modify their operations.

(v) Need for developing human resource: Indian enterprises have suffered for long with inadequately trained personnel. The new market conditions require people with higher competence and greater commitment. Hence the need for developing human resources.

(vi) Market orientation: Earlier firms used to produce first and go to the market for sale later. In other words, they had production oriented marketing operations. In a fast changing world, there is a shift to market orientation in as much as the firms have to study and analyse the market first and produce goods accordingly.

Meaning of business environment: The term business environment means the totality of all individuals, institutions and other forces that are outside a business but that potentially affect its performance. Business environment can be characterised in terms of

(a) totality of external forces

(b) specific and general forces

(c) inter-relatedness

(d) dynamic nature

_____

(e) uncertainty

(f) complexity

(g) relativity

Importance of business environment: Business environment and its understanding are important for (i) enabling the identification of opportunities and getting the first mover advantage, (ii) helping in the identification of threats and early warning signals, (iii) coping with the rapid changes, (v) assisting in planning and policy and (vi) improving the performance. (vii) Loss of budgetary support to the public sector: The central government's budgetary support for financing the public sector outlays has declined over the years. The public sector undertakings have realised that, in order to survive and grow, they will have to be more efficient and generate their own resources for the purpose.

On the whole, the impact of Government policy changes particularly in respect of liberalisation, privatisation and globalisation has been positive as the Indian business and industry has shown great resilience in dealing with the new economic order. Indian enterprises have developed strategies and adopted business processes and procedures to meet the challenge of competition. They have become more customer-focused and adopted measures to improve customer relationship and satisfaction.

Elements of business environment: Business environment consists of five important dimensions including economic, social, technological, political and legal.

Economic environment includes such factors as interest rates, inflation rates, changes in disposable income of people, stock market indexes and the value of rupee. Social environment includes social forces like traditions, values, social trends, society's expectations of business, and so on.

Technological environment includes forces relating to scientific improvements and innovations which provide new ways of producing goods and services and new methods and techniques of operating a business.

Political environment includes political conditions such as general stability and peace in the country and specific attitudes that elected government representatives hold toward business.

Legal environment includes various legislations passed by the government, administrative orders issued by government authorities, court judgments as well as decisions rendered by various commissions and agencies at every level of the government—center, state or local.

Economic environment in India: The economic environment in India consists of various macro-level factors related to the means of production and distribution of wealth which have an impact on business and industry. The economic environment of business in India has been steadily changing since Independence mainly due to government policies. In order to solve economic problems of our country at the time of Independence, the government took several steps including control by the state of key industries, central

———————

planning and reduced importance of the private sector. These steps delivered mixed results until 1991 when Indian economy happened to face serious foreign exchange crisis, high government deficit and a rising trend of prices despite bumper crops.

Liberalisation, privatisation and globalisation: As a part of economic reforms, the Government of India announced a new industrial policy in July 1991 which sought to liberate the industry from the shackles of the licensing system (liberalisation), drastically reduce the role of the public sector (privatisation) and encourage foreign private participation in industrial development (globalisation).

———————